Silver Ship

Sheila K. McCullagh

WIRRAL
EDUCATION COMMITTEE
ST. ALBAN'S R.C. SCHOOL
WALLASEY

Illustrated by
Derek Collard

Nelson

It was getting dark. The pavement was crowded with people hurrying home. Nicholas walked along slowly, with his hands in his pockets. Every now and then, he stopped and looked back. He saw only the dark, grey sky hanging down over the roofs of the houses, the lighted windows of the shops, and the crowd of people hurrying home. But he couldn't help feeling that something was going to happen.

He turned off the main road and down the side street which led to the house where he had lived for the past three years. (He still didn't call it 'home'.) As he opened the front door, a door opened on the landing over his head, and he saw his grandfather looking down at him from the top of the stairs.

"Nicholas! Come up here a minute," his grandfather said. He spoke softly, as if he didn't want anyone else to hear him.

Nicholas ran up the stairs two steps at a time, to the back bedroom where his grandfather lived.

The old man never went out these days. "What is there to go out for?" he always said, when anyone asked him.

"There's nothing to look at, now that we don't live by the sea. Who wants to look at cars going by? It was different when we lived by the harbour wall, and saw all the ships."

Nicholas missed the sea almost as much as his grandfather did. His grandfather had been a sailor, and Nicholas had been born by the sea. His father had been a sailor too – until he was drowned one night in a storm. Three years ago, Nicholas's mother had married again, and they had come to live in the town with his new step-father. His step-father already had two sons. They were both older than Nicholas and they had never even seen the sea.

"Come in a minute, Nicholas," said his grandfather. "I've something to tell you – and something to show you, too."

Nicholas followed the old man into the little room. It was as neat as a cabin in a ship, and not very much bigger. There was a neat bed against one wall, with a table beside it. There was an old wooden armchair in front of the fire.

The whole room looked bright and welcoming. There was a tall lamp by the chair, and it lit up the old sea charts on the wall. A ship's compass stood on the shelf over the fire, with a little sailing ship in a glass bottle beside it. One wall of the room was lined with books. A picture of an old cargo boat hung over the bed.

"Come and sit down, Nick," said his grandfather, waving his hand towards a low stool on the other side of the fire. "I've got some news for you. Your great-uncle Jeremy is dead. He's been lost at sea, far away on the other side of the world. He must have gone over the side of the ship in a storm. They went to his cabin, and there was no one there. They searched the ship, but they couldn't find him. Well, if he had to die, that was the way he wanted to go. Jeremy loved the sea."

Nicholas tried to remember Great-Uncle Jeremy. He had come to see them once, when his father was alive, when Nicholas was a very small boy. Nicholas could just remember a strange man with black eyes and thick white hair. Great-Uncle Jeremy had told Nicholas all kinds of strange tales about ships and the sea.

"Your great-uncle Jeremy was my eldest brother," his grandfather went on, staring into the fire. "He travelled all over the world, did my brother Jeremy. And he took a fancy to you. Do you remember? He said you'd be another just like him. And now he's dead. I had a letter this morning. He's sent you a picture. He left it to you in his will. It's there by the bed."

He nodded towards a narrow wooden box leaning up against the wall. "It was addressed to me, so I opened it. There was his watch inside, for me, and the picture for you. It's a strange picture. You get it out and have a look at it."

Nicholas opened the box and took out the picture. It was set in a black frame. He propped it up against the bed and sat down again on the stool to look at it.

It was a very strange picture indeed. Nicholas found himself looking at a wide, silvery-white ring. In the middle of the ring, a silvery-white ship was riding at anchor on a silvery-white sea. The sky was black, with silver stars, and all the rest of the picture outside the ring was deep black too. But the ship looked beautiful. It looked as if it were made of glass or silver, with the moon shining on it. Nicholas couldn't take his eyes off it.

"Ah!" said his grandfather, who was watching him. "My brother Jeremy knew what he was doing, when he left that picture to you. No one else would want it, but you or me, and it's right that you should have it."

"Don't you want it yourself?" asked Nicholas.

His grandfather shook his head. "Your great-uncle Jeremy left it to you, not me," he said. "And I think he was right. There's something strange about that picture. I don't know what it is, but I think I'm too old for it. Anyway, the picture's yours. I've got my ship, up there on the wall. She's good enough for me." He jerked his head towards the picture over the bed. "You take it, boy," he said. "Take it up to your room now, before the others see it. They won't like it, and there's no need for them to know about it. Off you go."

Nicholas took the picture and went up to his room. The house was a narrow one, and his room was in the attics. There was a nail on the wall, opposite the window. He hung the picture on that. He could look at it there when he was lying in bed.

The black of the picture stood out against the white wall of the attic. He looked at the ship closely. She was a sailing ship, the kind of ship men sailed in long ago. The sails were rolled up, and lashed to the spars, and the ship had a figure-head: there was a great silver creature jutting out over the water. "It's a great fish," Nicholas said to himself. "No it isn't. It's a dolphin – a silver dolphin." He sat looking at it until his mother called up from below, to tell him that supper was ready. Even when he put the light out to go downstairs, Nicholas could see the ship shining in the light of the street lamp outside.

Nicholas ate his supper with the others as usual. His grandfather always had supper up in his room. Grandfather hadn't told the others about Great-Uncle Jeremy and Nicholas said nothing about the picture. Even his mother never went up to his room, unless he was ill, so no one was likely to see it.

Nicholas was thinking about the picture most of the evening, and he felt strangely excited when he went up to bed. He took an apple up with him, as he always did, but he was too excited to finish it. He left it, half-eaten, on the table. He undressed, slipped into his pyjamas, and put out the light. He pulled back the curtains, and got quickly into bed. He lay there, looking at the ship. The ship was shining in the light of the street lamp, as if it had been made of silver. He wondered where Great-Uncle Jeremy had found the picture, and what ship it was, and where it had sailed. The ship had a strange look about it, as if it sailed on strange seas.

Nicholas lay there, watching the ship, until at last he fell asleep.

When Nicholas woke up, it was still dark. The street lamp had gone out, and the moonlight was streaming into the room. He looked across at the picture. The wide ring around the ship shone like white fire. The crests of the waves were shining with splashes of silver. As Nicholas gazed at the ship, it seemed to him that the ship was moving, rolling at anchor on the dark, moon-splashed sea.

As he watched, the ring of silver seemed to be growing bigger and bigger. So did the ship.

Nicholas climbed out of bed and moved across the room towards the picture. The ring of white fire seemed to be all around him. He felt as if he were stepping right through it. His bare feet left the floorboards behind, and stepped on to bare rock. He took another step forwards, and found himself in a cave, walking towards the moonlit sea.

There was sand under his feet now, and he could hear the waves, breaking on the rocks. He came to the end of the cave, and looked out.

He was looking out on to a moonlit beach. In front of him, sand and rocks sloped down to where the waves were breaking on the shore in a rush of white water. The ship he had seen in the picture rode at anchor in the bay. She was no longer silver, but a strong wooden ship. Only her sails and the dolphin on her prow still showed white under the moon.

Nicholas glanced down at himself. He was wearing a white shirt, open at the neck, and a pair of blue trousers that fastened below the knee. His legs and feet were bare.

He looked up, and saw a great rock jutting up out of the sand on his right. The sky shone light above it, as if there were a fire on the sands. He could hear shouting and singing coming from the far side. He made his way down the beach, along the great rock. It ended just above the breaking waves. Nicholas turned the corner of the rock, and stood still, staring.

Two boats were pulled up on the sand, and a great fire was blazing on the beach. All around the fire, men were sitting or lying on the sand. Most of them were eating and drinking, shouting and singing, but he could see about twenty men lying at one side, with their hands tied behind them.

One man was sitting propped up against a rock, with his arms bound to his sides. There were some strips of meat hanging from a frame in the smoke over the fire.

As Nicholas stood there, staring, one of the men saw him, and gave a great shout. In a moment, the others were on their feet. Each man drew a cutlass. Two of them rushed towards Nicholas, and for a moment he thought that they were going to cut him down. But one of them gripped his arm, twisted it behind his back, and pushed him forward into the firelight. The second man peered around the rock, the way Nicholas had come.

Nicholas found himself standing in front of a man who was sitting on a low rock at one side of the fire. The man was wearing a dark red coat, and a white shirt that looked as if it were made of silk. His head was bare, and he had dark hair and a short, pointed beard. He wore a gold ring on his finger and a heavy gold chain around his neck, hanging down over his shirt.

He looked Nicholas up and down, and then laughed.

"You've caught a sprat this time, Sharkey," he said. "He's not big enough to give us much trouble. Are there any more of them, Nim?"

"There's no one else that I can see," said the second man, coming back to the fire.

"He must be another ship's boy," said the man called Sharkey, giving Nicholas's arm a jerk.

Nicholas caught his breath with pain. But he wasn't going to cry out, if he could help it.

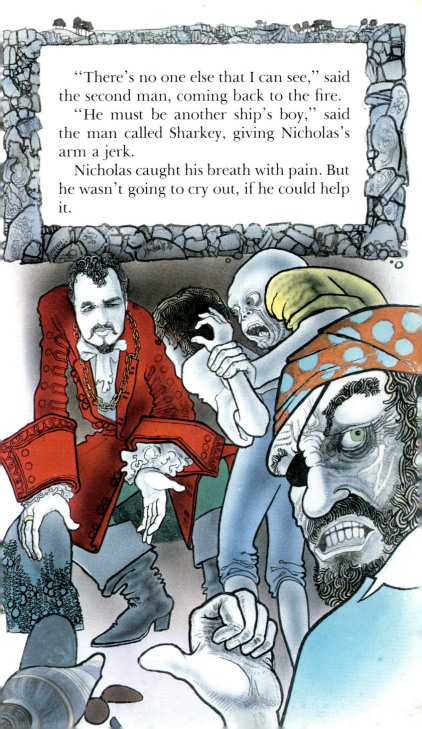

The man with the gold chain looked hard at Nicholas.

"Are you alone?" he asked.

"Yes," said Nicholas.

"I don't trust him, Cap'n Rasha," said Sharkey, giving his arm another jerk. "Where's he been hiding? That's what I'd like to know. If there's one of them, there may be more."

"Nip round that rock and take a good look, Quick Johnny," said the man called Captain Rasha.

A little, dark-haired seaman with a cheerful face picked up a lantern and lit it from the fire. He went off round the rock with the lantern in one hand and a cutlass in the other.

"We'll soon know," said Captain Rasha. "If anyone's there, Quick Johnny will find him."

Quick Johnny came back. "No one there, Cap'n," he said. "And only one set of footprints on the beach. He's been hiding in a cave."

Nicholas saw the man who was propped up against the rock lift his head suddenly, and look at him. The man opened his mouth as if he were going to speak, but he shut it again without saying anything. No one but Nicholas noticed.

"Well," said Captain Rasha. "You don't look as if you could do us any harm. We may even try to make a buccaneer out of you. We can do with a ship's boy. Toss him down with the others, Sharkey."

"Shall I tie him up?" asked Sharkey.

"There's no need to do that. We'll be going off to the ship soon, and he can make himself useful."

"Over there, then," said Sharkey, flinging Nicholas sideways suddenly, so that he fell at the feet of the man propped against the rock.

The others laughed. They pushed their cutlasses back into their belts, and picked up their drinking horns again.

Captain Rasha got up and strolled over to the rock where the bound man was sitting.

"Well, Francis Harken," he said softly. "I'll ask you once more. Why don't you join us? The Dragon Men will soon rule the Ocean of Ramir. Sail under their flag. You'll sail your ship as a free man, and be paid in good yellow gold!"

"No one who works for the Dragon Men is a free man, Rasha," the bound man said. "If you don't know that now, you'll find out before long. I sail my ship under the flag of my own country, the country of

Ramir. We came here to look for the Dragon Men, and so did you – to fight them, not to join them."

"You're a fool, Captain Harken," said Captain Rasha. "You've no choice in the matter. You can sail your ship under the Dragon flag, and fight for the Dragon Men – or you can pull an oar for them in one of their galleys, as a galley slave. You'll work for them, one way or the other. You've no choice. You're one of the best sailors I know. We're both buccaneers – sea-rovers. Join us as a sea-rover, not as a galley slave!"

"You're no longer a sea-rover, Rasha," said Captain Harken. "You're a sea-robber! Or should I call you a sea-dog – one of the dogs of the Dragon Men?"

"Dogs are we?" cried Sharkey. "I'll teach you to call us dogs!" He picked up a blazing stick from the fire and pushed it into Captain Harken's face.

Before the stick could touch Captain Harken, Nicholas flung himself at Sharkey. He knocked the blazing wood out of his hand, and it fell to the ground on Sharkey's foot.

There was a yell of pain from Sharkey, and the next moment Nicholas was knocked spinning sideways by a blow from Nim. He fell against a rock. Nim kicked him, knocking all the breath out of his body. He had lifted his foot back to kick him again, when Captain Rasha's voice stopped him.

"That'll do, Nim," he said. "Don't kill him. We need a ship's boy. You can teach him manners later."

"I'll do that all right," said Nim under his breath. "I'll teach him with the rope's end!"

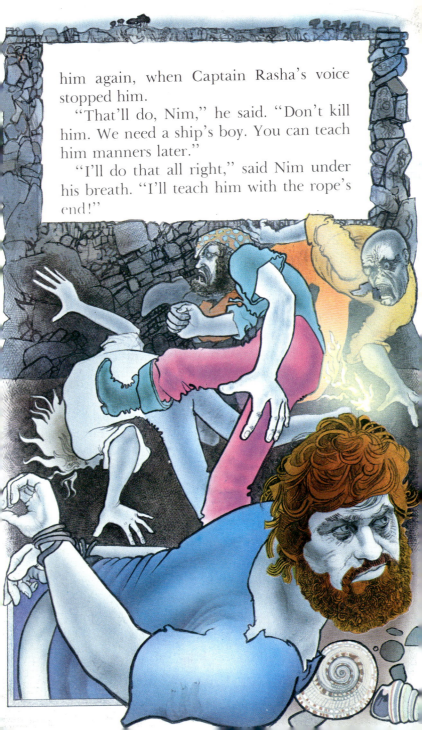

Nicholas lay gasping on the sand, trying to get his breath back. He stared up at Nim, and Nim stared back at him. He was a fierce looking man, with a black patch over one eye, and a white scar on his cheek. Nicholas felt sick. He rolled over and tried to get to his feet.

"Take your time, boy, take your time," said a deep voice near him. He looked up and saw one of the prisoners smiling at him. He was a very big man with thick red hair and a red beard. "I'd lie still for a bit, if I were you," the man said, giving him a nod. Nicholas nodded back. He had no breath to speak. Sharkey was nursing his foot and cursing at one side of the fire. Nicholas knew that he had better keep out of Sharkey's way.

Captain Rasha was still standing in front of Captain Harken, looking down at him.

"You should be more careful what you say, Harken," he said softly. "Sharkey doesn't like being called names, nor do the rest of us. Well, you'll have three days to think it over, while we sail to the Islands of the South. Then you'll work for the Dragon Men – as a free buccaneer, or as a galley slave. I'm giving you the choice, because we've worked together and sailed together in the old days. You'll be a fool if you don't take the chance I'm giving you."

He turned to the seamen.

"All right men," he said. "Pack up. We'll get back on board for the night, and sail in the morning. Sharkey, you take ten men off to *The Silver Dolphin*. The rest of you come with me. We'll take the prisoners on board *The Golden Dragon*!"

There was a general packing up on the sands. The strips of meat which had been drying over the fire were packed into baskets and slung on two carrying poles. Two small barrels of rum were slung beside them. Four sailors picked up the ends of the poles.

"Put that rum in the boat for *The Golden Dragon*," Captain Rasha said. "I don't want you drinking all night on *The Silver Dolphin*."

Nicholas heard Sharkey curse under his breath, but he didn't say anything aloud.

The prisoners were jerked to their feet and pushed along towards the boats. Nim gave Nicholas a clip on the back of his head, to drive him forward with the rest. He stumbled across the sand, keeping as close to Captain Harken as he could.

The prisoners were pushed into one of the boats, and made to lie down on the floor. Ten or eleven sailors ran the boat into the water, and then climbed in. They kicked the prisoners out of the way of their feet, sat down, and took the oars. They held the boat steady in the water, while Captain Rasha stepped in. Then they pulled out into the waves.

Nicholas was the only prisoner not tied up. He crouched down in the bows, trying to keep out of everyone's way. He looked back towards the island. Sharkey and the rest of the sailors had run the second boat down into the sea and were climbing into it.

Nicholas looked ahead. He thought that they were going out to the ship at anchor in the bay, but they rowed past it, under the prow of the boat. Nicholas looked up and saw the silver dolphin shining in the moonlight.

As they came around the point, Nicholas saw that they were making for a rocky cove. Another ship lay at anchor there. The moonlight was very bright and the night was clear. There was a big dragon, carved out of wood and painted gold, on the prow of the ship. A lantern was swinging on the prow, and another at the ship's stern. There were lights on board, too, and Nicholas could see the gleam of a cannon, forward on the deck of the ship. A man hailed them from across the water.

Nim answered with a shout. The men at the oars pulled the boat in. A ladder lay against the ship's side. The men climbed up. The prisoners were half dragged, half carried on board, and thrown down on the deck. Nicholas climbed up with the seamen.

Captain Rasha swung himself over the side. He looked down at his prisoners.

"Cut the ropes and put them in irons. Get them down below," he said. "A few days down there, and they'll be glad to join us. Leave both the boys on deck. They can start to make themselves useful. They won't run away. There's nowhere for them to run to."

Nicholas found himself pushed to one side. A boy about his own age was tossed down on the deck beside him. His hands were tied with a rope, and someone had tied his legs, so that he could only just walk. The buccaneers took the other prisoners below, to put them in irons.

Captain Rasha went into a big cabin under the poop deck. Nim came across the deck with a pitcher of water, a basket of bread and a lantern.

"Here," he said, giving the basket to Nicholas. "Come down with me. This is for the prisoners. The Captain wants to keep them healthy. He'll get a better price for them."

He led Nicholas down some steps into the ship. Lanterns were swinging from the great beams, and there were men everywhere. They went across a space piled with sacks and barrels. They came to a heavy wooden door, with a bar across it.

Nim set down the pitcher and lifted the bar. "In there," he said, opening the door. Nicholas went in. He set the basket down, and Nim handed him the pitcher. "Give them a drink, and a hunk of bread. I'll come back for you later," he said. "No tricks, mind! If you give any trouble, you'll get a taste of the rope's end! And of my boot, too!"

He shut the door, and Nicholas heard the bar drop into place. He set down the pitcher, and lifted the lantern.

He was standing in a small space in the bows of the ship, walled off from the rest. Captain Harken and the others were lying on the floor where the seamen had thrown them. Their hands and feet were fastened with iron bands.

Captain Harken turned to look at Nicholas.

"Hang up the lantern, boy," he said. "Then we'll see where we are."

Nicholas looked up, and saw a hook in a beam above his head. He lifted up the lantern, and hung it from the hook. It hung there, swinging gently with the movement of the ship, and sending black shadows dancing on the walls.

"Help us to get propped up against the side, boy," said Captain Harken. "Then we'll have a drink of water and a bit of that bread. We can do with it."

Nicholas helped each man to pull himself against the wall. There wasn't much room, but Nicholas did the best he could, and soon they were all sitting more comfortably. He took the pitcher round and gave each of them a drink and a hunk of bread from the basket. They ate as if they were very hungry.

"Well, boy, and where did you spring from?" asked the big man with red hair.

"I – I came from the cave," stammered Nicholas.

"And how did you get into the cave?" asked the man.

"I'm – I'm not sure," stammered Nicholas.

"Not sure!" cried the big man. "Not sure!"

"Leave the boy alone, Barnabas Brandy," said Captain Harken. "You're not one of Rasha's men, are you boy? What's your name?"

"Nicholas. And I've never seen Captain Rasha, till tonight."

Captain Harken nodded. "I thought so," he said. "Have you heard of the land of Ramir?"

Nicholas shook his head.

"Ah!" said Captain Harken. "I thought as much. I've met your kind before. Well, Nicholas, you've earned my thanks tonight. Sharkey was in an ugly mood. Keep away from him, if you can."

"He's on the other ship," said Nicholas.

"*The Silver Dolphin*," said Captain Harken. "She's our ship, *The Silver Dolphin*."

"I hope he falls off into the sea, and the sharks get him!" added Barnabas Brandy.

The door behind Nicholas opened and Nim looked in.

"All right, that's it," he said. "Come on out. Bring the lantern with you. They can sit there in the dark and think about it. It will do them good."

Nicholas pushed the last hunk of bread into his shirt. He unhooked the lantern, and came out with the empty basket. Nim took the jug.

"Up on deck with you!" said Nim.

The other boy was lying on the deck where they had left him, still tied up. Nim kicked him.

"You can untie him and sleep here," he said roughly to Nicholas. "And don't try anything on, or I'll toss you overboard. We're going to put out to sea."

He stamped off into the darkness.

"Let me get those ropes off," said

Nicholas, dropping down on the deck beside the boy.

The boy stared at him for a moment, and then held out his hands.

All around them, the buccaneers were climbing up the rigging, getting the ship ready to sail. They heard Captain Rasha shout something, and then the rattle of the anchor against the side of the ship.

The deck tilted a little, the sails filled, and the ship began to move.

Nicholas began work on the ropes around the boy's wrists.

"You're not one of Rasha's men, are you?" asked the boy. He was about Nicholas's age, or a year older.

"I've never seen Captain Rasha before tonight," said Nicholas. "Turn your hands over a bit, so that I can get at that knot. What's your name?"

"Halek. What's yours?"

"Nicholas."

"What have they done with Captain Harken and the others?"

"They're down below," said Nicholas. "They're in a sort of cabin – a prison – in the bows of the ship. They put them in irons. There – that's your hands free. They gave me some bread for the prisoners, and I saved a hunk for us. You can eat your half, while I get the ropes off your legs."

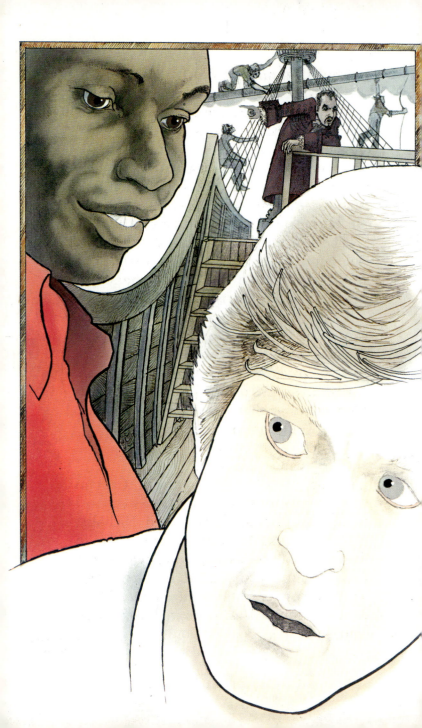

Halek took the bread in both hands and took a bite.

"Where do you come from?" asked Nicholas, working away at the ropes. "And how did Captain Rasha take you prisoner?"

"We're from Ramir," said Halek.

"Where's that?" asked Nicholas.

"You must know Ramir," said Halek in surprise. "This is the Ocean of Ramir. Ramir is the country away over there, far to the south and west of us. Three years ago, strange things began to happen. Ships set out from Ramir and were never heard of again. At first we thought they'd been lost at sea in storms. But then we began to hear strange stories – tales of the Dragon Men. There have always been tales of the Dragon Men in Ramir. It's said that they come from a city of gold. Haven't you heard of them?"

Nicholas shook his head. "I know nothing about them at all," he said. "What happened then?"

"A year ago, three ships of buccaneers set out from Ramir, to find out the truth of it all," said Halek. "Rasha was captain of one of them, but his ship wasn't called *The Golden Dragon* then – she was *The Golden Rose*. Then there was a ship called *The Blue Whale*. And there was *The Silver Dolphin*. That's our ship.

"The buccaneers have always fought the enemies of Ramir. In good times, we live by trading among the islands. But if anyone attacks Ramir, then we fight. Captain Rasha was always looking for gold, too. When we heard that the Dragon Men had been seen among the islands, we all set out to look for them.

"*The Silver Dolphin* has been sailing among the islands for a year now. We've been trading fish and dried meat, and picking up tales about the Dragon Men. But we haven't seen them, and we couldn't find anyone who has. There were plenty of stories about them, but no one knew where they were. I expect we'll find out now.

"We'd seen nothing of Rasha, or of *The Blue Whale*, until today. We came in to the bay at dawn. We didn't see *The Golden Dragon*. She was hidden in the cove.

"We went on shore, to shoot the wild goats for meat, as we often do in the islands. We'd just got the fire going on the beach, when Rasha's men came over the rocks. We thought they were friends. We were <u>glad</u> to see them! The traitors!

"Captain Harken asked them for news of the Dragon Men. They gave us news of the Dragon Men, all right! They'd met the Dragon Men in the Islands of the South –

sold themselves to them for gold! They're all traitors, every one of them. Before we knew what had happened, their knives were at our throats. We hadn't a chance. There were two of them for every one of us.

"So they tied us up. They've been laughing at us all day long. Rasha tried to make Captain Harken say he'd join the Dragon Men too. Captain Harken isn't a traitor. He'd sink *The Silver Dolphin* first! And I believe that Rasha doesn't care if we join them or not. The Dragon Men's ships are galleys. They need galley slaves to row at the oars. Galley slaves don't live long, when they row for the Dragon Men. Rasha wants gold, and the Dragon Men have plenty of gold, by all accounts. Rasha will sell us as slaves to the Dragon Men, and then he'll laugh. How he'll laugh! I hope he dies laughing!"

"Rasha's not going to sell you, even if he sells the others," said Nicholas. "He's going to keep you on *The Golden Dragon*. He's going to keep me, too. He said something about making us buccaneers. Move your left leg a bit, so that I can get at that knot."

"I'd rather die in the galleys with Captain Harken, than stay on *The Golden Dragon*," cried Halek. "Buccaneers! They're not buccaneers. Buccaneers are sea-rovers, like us. You heard what Captain Harken called them. They're not sea-rovers. They're sea-dogs – the dogs of the Dragon Men!"

Nicholas pulled the last bit of rope clear.

"Well, you're free now, anyway," he said.

Halek moved his legs slowly, and bent down to rub them.

"I'll jump in the sea and swim for it, rather than join them!" he cried fiercely.

"Sh!" said Nicholas. "Don't shout! It's no good jumping just now. The island is a long way off already. We'll stay with the ship till we're near an island. Then we'll both slip over the side together."

"I'll not leave the ship, while Captain Harken is on board," said Halek, still rubbing his legs. "But thanks for setting me free. I shan't forget."

"What happened to *The Blue Whale?*" asked Nicholas, taking out his bread and beginning to eat it.

"We haven't seen her since we left Ramir," said Halek. "Rasha didn't say anything about her. The Dragon Men may have sunk her – or she may be in the islands. The buccaneers on her haven't joined Rasha. He'd have told us if they had."

The door of the great cabin opened and Nim came out. He strode over to them.

"The Captain says you'll be safer below decks for the night," he said, roughly. "Down with you!" He aimed a kick at Halek, who was still stiff and who moved slowly. Nicholas sprang up and pulled Halek to his feet.

"Down there!" shouted Nim, pointing to the hatch.

They climbed down and found themselves in the big space in the forward part of the ship. It was crowded with seamen, who were busy slinging their hammocks for the night.

A lantern swung from a beam overhead, and Nicholas and Halek made their way over to the prison in the bows of the ship.

A buccaneer was standing guard by the door leading to the prison, where Captain Harken and his men were lying. The boys found a space at the side. Halek lay down to sleep.

Nicholas was very tired. He felt sure that he would never sleep on the hard boards of the rolling ship, but he dropped down beside Halek. He heard the wooden beams of the ship creaking and groaning around him. He heard the rush of the waves on the ship's side, as the ship's bows cut through the water. Nicholas closed his eyes. The next moment, he was asleep.

He woke up to find Nim kicking him. He struggled to his feet. It still seemed dark in the ship, but it was daylight outside. Nicholas and Halek struggled up on deck.

The ship was flying before the wind, with all her sails set. There were no islands in sight – nothing but the tossing waves and the blue sea, and *The Silver Dolphin* sailing behind them. A seaman pushed a mop into his hands, and threw a leather bucket at his head. Halek had a leather bucket too, and they began to mop the deck.

The next three days seemed like some kind of nightmare to Nicholas. And yet he was excited, and sometimes even happy, to find himself at sea.

Nim kicked them awake each morning. They mopped the decks, and waited on Captain Rasha in the great cabin. Captain Rasha lived in the cabin, with two other buccaneers: Marcus, the second mate, and Cram, the bo'sun. Halek and Nicholas took their meals along from the ship's galley each day. They waited on them, while they ate. They cleaned the cabin, and ran messages. By the time night fell, they were so tired that they fell asleep as soon as they dropped down on the boards by the prison.

Nim was in charge of the seamen on the lower deck. He kicked Nicholas and Halek, or cuffed them, whenever they went near him. "To teach them manners," he said. They kept as clear of him as they could. Twice a day, they took a big jug of water, and another of thick soup, to the prisoners. There was a basket of hunks of dark brown bread for them, too. Nim always went with them, and stood in the doorway while the prisoners ate. He didn't give them another chance to talk.

Nicholas and Halek had the same food themselves, afterwards. It was good soup. Captain Rasha wanted to keep his prisoners healthy. He wanted to get a good price for them, from the Dragon Men.

They had a fair wind, and the ship sailed well.

There was always one seaman up in the crow's-nest, high up on the mast. Towards the end of the third day, the look-out in the crow's-nest cried: "Land ho!" Just before sunset, they came to the Islands of the South.

Nicholas and Halek had been working below decks, cleaning up. It wasn't until they heard the anchor chain running out that they were able to go up on deck and see where they were.

They found the ship anchored just off a tall rock, which stuck up out of the sea at the end of the island, like a black tower. Another, much larger, island lay to the south and east of them, across a channel of water. A little bay, with golden sands, stretched from the tower rock to a big hill at the far end of the little island. The rocks and islands looked black and bare, except for some kind of green trees or bushes that grew beyond the sands along the bay. The flag at the masthead scarcely moved in the light wind, and the sky and the sea were a clear blue-green.

But Halek and Nicholas scarcely glanced at the sea and the islands. They were staring at a ship, which was pulling out towards them from the big island across the channel of water.

It was a galley. There was a mast, but the big sail was roped down, and the galley was being pulled across by oars. The prow of the galley was a great golden dragon, with wings which stretched back along the ship's sides. There was a platform at the stern with a small cannon on it. There was a red post at each corner and a red roof over it. Golden dragons were carved on the posts, and painted on the roof.

A Dragon Man stood on the platform at the stern of the galley, steering with a big steering oar.

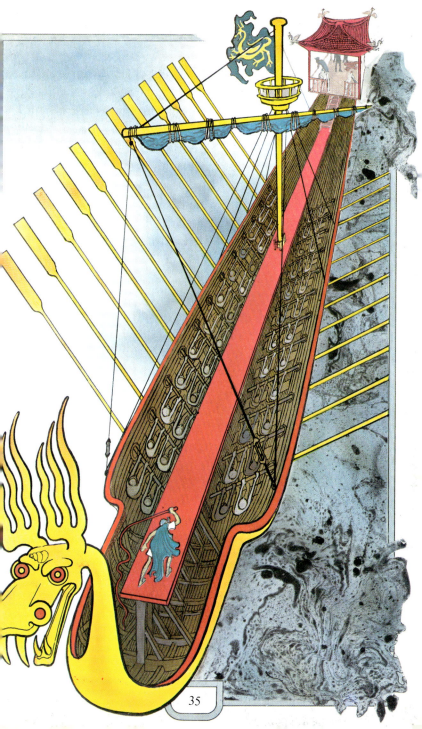

35

There were four or five other Dragon Men with him. Each wore a head-dress, or helmet, made of small metal plates, that looked like scales. The scales hung down from the helmet over their shoulders like a cape. All the men wore white and golden-coloured sandals. One man had a red helmet; the helmets of the other men were a greeny-blue. Every helmet had the same crest: a golden dragon with its wings back, ready to fly.

A long, narrow platform ran down the middle of the galley. The galley slaves sat on each side of it, chained to the oars. A Dragon Man walked up and down the long platform, with a long whip in his hand.

The galley pulled alongside *The Golden Dragon*. The man with the red helmet climbed on board. His white tunic had golden bands on it. There was a golden cord around his waist, and bands of gold on his arms. A long knife in a red sheath hung from the golden cord. He seemed to be the captain of the galley. Two other Dragon Men followed him and waited, standing just behind him.

Captain Rasha came out of the great cabin to greet the Dragon Captain. He lifted his hand in greeting, and the Dragon Man nodded his head in reply.

"I've captured a ship for the Dragon

King," said Captain Rasha, pointing to *The Silver Dolphin*, which had anchored near them. "I've a crew of my own men on board. I've twenty seamen to sell you, too, as slaves for your galleys."

The Dragon Captain glanced across at *The Silver Dolphin*. Nicholas saw his eyes light up. He was clearly excited at the sight of the ship. But he checked himself, and spoke coldly to Captain Rasha.

"Good," he said. "We need ships and we need slaves. Where are the men?"

Captain Rasha turned to Nim.

"Take off their leg-irons and bring them on deck," he said.

The Dragon Captain waited silently while Nim went below. Then Captain Harken and his men climbed up through the hatch on to the deck, with Nim behind them. The irons were still on their wrists, but their legs were free.

Nim lined them up and the Dragon Captain walked slowly along the line, looking at them. Then he turned to Captain Rasha.

"They'll do," he said coldly. "I will give you five gold coins for each man, except the old man." He pointed to one of the seamen, who had white hair. "He won't live long at the oars. You can have three gold coins for him."

"I'll take ten gold coins for each of them," said Captain Rasha, leaning back against the rail of the ship. "No more and no less. These men are all seamen. They'll make good galley slaves."

The Dragon Captain's head went up, and he stared at Captain Rasha with an angry look.

"You will get no more than I have said," he answered coldly. "If you are wise, you will take it. It is never wise to make the Dragon King angry."

"The Dragon King knows how useful I am to him," said Captain Rasha, with a smile. "I've captured a ship, and I shall be able to serve the Dragon King even better with two ships than I could with one. I'm sure the Dragon King will tell you that you have offered me too little. I am offering good seamen to you as galley slaves. I want ten gold coins for each man. Take my message to the Dragon King. I'll stay here at anchor till tomorrow, to wait for his reply."

The Dragon Captain stared at Captain Rasha for a moment without speaking. He was white with anger. Then he turned on his heel and went back over the side to the galley, with his two men.

Captain Rasha stood leaning against the rail, watching, as the galley pulled back towards the big island.

"Well, Marcus," he said, with his eyes still on the galley, "I don't think the Dragon King often gets a message like that. But I'm not one of his galley slaves, and we're the best seamen he's got. I think he'll give us our price."

"I don't know how you dare take the risk," said Marcus, shaking his head.

Captain Rasha laughed. "That's why I'm captain, and not you, Marcus," he cried, turning away from the rail. "I know when to take a risk, and when not to."

"I hope you're right," said Marcus.

"Of course he's right," cried Nim. "You're always right, Captain, aren't you? How about a barrel of rum for the men? We're safe in port, with a prize ship and a cargo of slaves. The men will want something for that."

Captain Rasha thought for a moment, and then nodded his head.

"Set a watch, Nim," he said. "No drink for the watchman, and no drink for the men on *The Silver Dolphin*. They can have it tomorrow night. We need one ship's crew wide awake, when we're anchored among the Dragon Men. But the rest of you can have rum. Bring some to the great cabin. I need it, too. Get the prisoners below again."

He strode back inside the great cabin, and Marcus followed him.

Nim took Captain Harken and his men below, and came up again a few minutes later.

"You take the watch, Quick Johnny," he said to the little man Nicholas had seen on the beach. "You're watchman for tonight. The rest of you get below. We'll make a night of it."

"Have I got to be on watch all night?" asked Quick Johnny.

"You can have your go at the rum tomorrow," said Nim. "You keep your eyes open tonight."

There was a hail from *The Silver Dolphin*. "How about a barrel of rum for us, Nim?" Sharkey shouted across the water. "There's no rum in this ship. We're safe in port. How about a barrel?"

"Not tonight," Nim shouted back. "Rum for us tonight, and for you tomorrow."

"We'll not put up with that, Nim!" shouted Sharkey. "We want that rum, and we want it now. I'm coming over."

"If you come over, you'll be sent back again," called Nim. "No rum for you tonight. Captain's orders. You'll have to put up with it."

He went down through the hatch after the others.

Nicholas saw Halek looking at him.

Halek jerked his head backwards towards the mast. Nim had forgotten them. The sun had gone, and the light was fading from the sky. They slipped behind the mast into the shadows.

"There's no need for us to go down there," whispered Halek. "Nim's forgotten us. They'll drink and shout half the night, and then they'll sleep. It'll be much better up on deck."

They made themselves as comfortable as they could among some ropes. They could hear shouts from below already. Someone began to sing, and other voices joined in.

They hadn't been settled down long, when they heard a shout from the water near the ship.

"Nim!" It was Sharkey's voice. "Nim! Where's that barrel of rum?"

Quick Johnny ran across to the ship's rail and looked down. Sharkey was just below, with two seamen, in *The Silver Dolphin's* boat.

"Don't make such a row, Sharkey!" called Quick Johnny softly. "Nim's below. I'll lower a barrel of rum down to you. I've got one up here on deck. But don't make such a row about it. Captain Rasha said you weren't to have any drink on *The Silver Dolphin* tonight."

"Captain Rasha's mad, if he thinks we'll sit over there doing nothing," said Sharkey. "Lower away, Quick Johnny! You're the man for us!"

Quick Johnny rolled a barrel over to the side, and lowered it into the boat.

"Pull away!" he called softly.

"Pull away!" called Sharkey in reply.

Halek and Nicholas crept to the rail and looked over. The boat was pulling back to *The Silver Dolphin*.

They watched the men pull her into the dark shadow of the ship, and then they slipped back to the mast.

"I hope the Dragon Men don't attack us," whispered Halek, as they settled down. "They'll all be drunk on *The Silver Dolphin* in no time, now."

They lay awake, listening to the songs and shouting below, until at last their eyes closed, and they fell asleep.

Nicholas felt a hand gripping his foot. He opened his eyes, and saw Quick Johnny bending over him. Quick Johnny's finger was on his lips.

"Sh!" he said. "Don't make a sound."

"What is it?" whispered Nicholas, sitting up. "Is it the Dragon Men?"

He saw that Halek was awake too.

"No," whispered Quick Johnny. "There's no sign of them. But it's now or never, if you want to set Captain Harken free."

"What do you mean?" asked Halek. "You're one of Captain Rasha's men. You don't belong to *The Silver Dolphin*. It's a trick."

"Sh!" whispered Quick Johnny. "It's no trick. I belong to Ramir, and so do you, and so does Captain Harken. I shipped with Rasha, but I didn't have a choice. I was just out of jail, and no one else would have me. I don't mind Captain Rasha, but I'm not joining any Dragon Men. Rasha said we'd lay our hands on some of their gold. I don't mind that, but I'm not going to do it by selling men from Ramir to the Dragon Men as galley slaves. And I'm not going to fight against ships from Ramir."

"What are you going to do now, then?" whispered Nicholas.

"They're all drunk or sleeping on *The Golden Dragon*," said Quick Johnny. "They'll be the same way on *The Silver Dolphin*, too, by now. I've got the keys to the irons. First, we'll creep below and set Captain Harken and his men free. Then we'll take a boat over to *The Silver Dolphin*. They won't have set a watch on her tonight. They'll all be fast asleep by this time. We should be able to take the ship."

"How did you get the keys?" asked Halek. "Nim would never have given them to you."

"How do you think I got them?" said Quick Johnny softly. "I stole them, of course! I'm the best pickpocket in Ramir. Didn't you know? That's why I was in jail. I can pick a man's pocket so fast, he doesn't know what's happened."

"Someone must have known what happened, if you ended up in jail," said Halek.

"Ah, well, that's a long story," whispered Quick Johnny. "And there's no time to tell it now. You take the keys and go down and get Captain Harken and his men. They won't trust me, but they'll trust you. I'll stay on deck, in case anyone wakes up. The boat is tied alongside, all ready to go ashore in the morning."

"I'll stay with you," said Halek. "And if you make a sound, or call the others, I'll kill you!"

"Now why would I do that?" asked Quick Johnny. "It's my plan, isn't it?"

"I'll stay with you, just the same," said Halek. "You take the keys, Nick. I don't trust him."

Nicholas took the keys and went below. A lantern was swinging from a beam overhead and another lantern stood on the floor. No one was awake. There was a strong smell of rum, and men were lying about everywhere. Their drinking horns lay at their sides, where they had dropped them. Nicholas picked up the lantern, and made his way over to the door of the prison. There was no watchman beside it tonight.

Nicholas set down the lantern. He lifted the bar that held the door shut, and set it softly down on the deck. The door swung open. He picked up the lantern again and went inside. Captain Harken sat up and stared at him. Nicholas put his finger on his lips.

"What's to do?" he heard Barnabas Brandy whisper.

"Sh!" came Captain Harken's whisper in reply. All the men from *The Silver Dolphin* were awake now, and getting to their feet. Only their wrists were fastened. Nim hadn't bothered to put the leg-irons back when he shut them in again.

Barnabas Brandy took Nicholas's lantern, and held it in both hands, while Nicholas unlocked the iron bands around Captain Harken's wrists, and set them down on the boards at his feet. Then he went from man to man, setting them free. The last man was Barnabas Brandy.

"What now?" Captain Harken whispered.

"Quick Johnny was on watch on *The Golden Dragon*. He's on our side now," whispered Nicholas. "He stole the keys, and told me to set you free. He's on deck. Halek's with him. Everyone's asleep on *The Golden Dragon*. They've been drinking rum.

It's the same on *The Silver Dolphin*. Quick Johnny let them have a barrel of rum, too. There's a boat alongside."

"Then we'll take *The Silver Dolphin*," said Captain Harken softly.

"What about the men on this ship? Shall we tie them up?" asked Barnabas Brandy.

Captain Harken shook his head. "They might wake," he said. "Some of them could use their pistols. They're not all drunk. We haven't much time, if we're going to get away. Remember, the Dragon Men have galleys, and there isn't much wind. We'll take *The Silver Dolphin*, and sail her out to sea before they know what's happened. Come on."

He led the way to the ladder. The others followed like shadows, stepping over the sleeping sailors, hardly daring to breathe. But nobody woke, and they soon found themselves safely up on the deck.

Halek and Quick Johnny were waiting for them by the boat. One after another, they climbed down into it.

"Muffle your oars," whispered Captain Harken. The men pulled off the cloths that were round their necks, and muffled the oars.

"Pull away!" whispered Captain Harken.

The boat slid out from the side of *The Golden Dragon*, into the moonlight.

There was a light still burning in the great cabin, and the lantern shone out through the windows. There was a lantern on the stern of *The Silver Dolphin*, too. It shone out, as they rounded the stern of *The Golden Dragon*, and pulled across the path of moonlight and into the shadow of the ship.

Barnabas Brandy had taken the boat's tiller and Captain Harken stood beside him. They pulled alongside *The Silver Dolphin*. There was still no hail from the deck.

A rope ladder hung down the ship's side. Captain Harken gripped it and pulled himself up. He vanished silently over the rail. The others followed. Halek and Nicholas scrambled up after the men. Barnabas Brandy made the boat fast to the ship's side and followed them.

Nicholas found himself standing on the deck with the others. He saw an open hatch. Captain Harken made a sign to the boys to stay on deck. Then he slipped down through the hatch, followed by the others.

"We'll make sure there's no one asleep on deck," whispered Halek. "Then we must keep watch. Come on. Keep with me."

They crept forward. The deck was empty. Sharkey hadn't bothered to set a watch. He and all the other seamen were below.

Nicholas and Halek heard a muffled cry from the hatch, followed by a thud. Then more thuds sounded from below. There was a muffled shout. Then there was silence.

A head showed above the hatch, and Barnabas Brandy climbed out on deck. He saw the two boys.

"Got them!" he whispered with a chuckle. "We've got every last man of them. Tied them up like so many chickens! We've got their pistols, too, and their cutlasses. They'll do no harm now."

He chuckled again, and turned back to the hatch. Another seaman joined him, and they began hauling on a rope.

One after another, the seamen from *The Golden Dragon* were hauled up on deck. Some of them used their legs to help themselves. Some of them were hauled up like so many sacks of potatoes. They all had their hands tied behind them, and they were all gagged.

Sharkey came last. Nicholas could see by his eyes that he was awake. His eyes burned with rage, when he saw the boys. He looked so angry, that Nicholas took a step backwards.

Barnabas Brandy chuckled again. "Nothing to be frightened of," he said with a deep laugh. "He can't do any harm – not now. If I had my way, he never would. We'd drop him over the side. But Captain Harken won't do that. He's too soft-hearted."

Captain Harken came up on deck.

"Lower them into the boat," he whispered. "What are you waiting for, Barnabas? Lower them down just as they

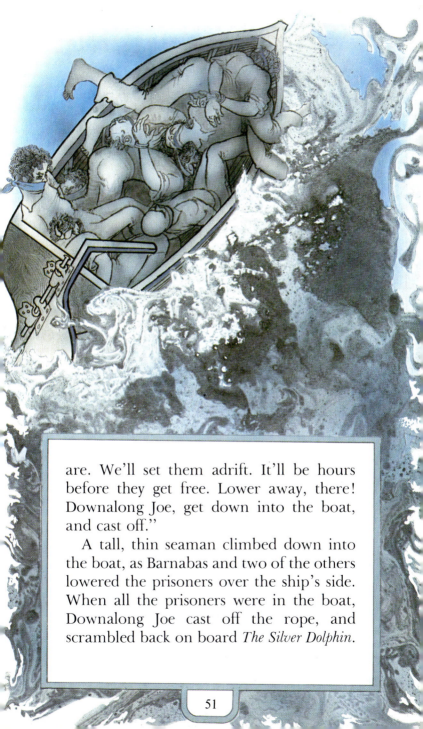

are. We'll set them adrift. It'll be hours before they get free. Lower away, there! Downalong Joe, get down into the boat, and cast off."

A tall, thin seaman climbed down into the boat, as Barnabas and two of the others lowered the prisoners over the ship's side. When all the prisoners were in the boat, Downalong Joe cast off the rope, and scrambled back on board *The Silver Dolphin*.

"Now – up anchor! Get those sails set, Barnabas! We shall need every one of them to catch this wind. Be as quiet as you can."

Nicholas saw the buccaneers climbing the rigging, letting out the sails. The anchor was hauled up. The lantern on the ship's stern was put out.

"Take the wheel, Martin Quinn," Captain Harken whispered to a dark, strange-looking man, who was standing near him. "We'll take her out to sea. We shall have to run before the wind. It's our only chance. If the Dragon Men see us, they'll send their galleys after us. They can travel faster than we can, unless it blows harder than this."

"They'll catch us, for sure, if they see us," said Downalong Joe.

"I'm not so sure about that," said Martin Quinn, moving over to the ship's wheel.

"We'll find more wind out to sea," said Barnabas Brandy. "There's a storm coming."

"They don't have storms in these islands," said Downalong Joe, shaking his head.

"Then they're in for a surprise," said Barnabas Brandy.

The ship swung slowly out to sea. There was still no sign that anyone was awake on *The Golden Dragon*. The wind grew stronger, as the ship got under way.

Nicholas stood by the ship's rail, watching the waves sweep along the sides of the ship. He wondered if the Dragon Men had set a watch on the ship.

There was a cry from the look-out in the crow's-nest.

"Galleys! Two galleys astern of us, just putting out from the big island!"

Nicholas looked back. Two galleys were sweeping out from the island towards them. Their sails were set to catch the wind and they were using their oars as well.

"They're gaining on us," cried the man in the crow's-nest.

"Light the stern lantern," said Captain Harken. "I want them to see us."

"They can see us easily enough in this moonlight, without that," Nicholas heard Downalong Joe mutter under his breath.

The light of the lantern shone out into the night.

"Stand by the guns!" cried Captain Harken.

There were two cannon on the deck of *The Silver Dolphin*, as there had been on *The Golden Dragon*. Four men ran forward to them.

"We'll never hit the galleys, in this light," muttered Downalong Joe.

"Hold your fire!" cried Captain Harken. "We'll fire if they close up on us. But there's a wind coming. Look at those clouds! We'll get away from them yet! North, north-east, Martin. Take her round the end of the big island."

"North, north-east it is," said Martin Quinn. The ship's wheel swung in his hands, and the ship turned half into the wind.

"We're losing way! They're closing the gap!" cried Downalong Joe.

"We'll lose them, too, in a minute," said Captain Harken. His eyes were on black clouds, which were beginning to blow up over the islands.

"Get that barrel of pitch up here, Tom Gold," called Captain Harken.

One of the seamen rolled a barrel of pitch over to the side of the ship. He tied one end of a rope around it, and stood waiting, holding the rest of the rope in his hands.

"Lower it over the side as we round the point," cried Captain Harken. "Get ready to light it, Tom. We'll cut it loose the moment we're out of sight. It'll drift away on the current. Keep the ship in under the cliffs, Martin. It's darkest there. We'll have to sail as close to the wind as we can."

The Silver Dolphin slid into the darkest shadows under the cliffs of the big island as she rounded the point, and turned half into the wind. They were out of sight of the galleys.

"Now!" cried Captain Harken. "Put that lantern out, Downalong Joe! Light the tar barrel, Tom! Cut it loose!"

Downalong Joe put out the stern lantern. Tom Gold dropped a flaming torch into the barrel of tar, and cut it loose. It floated away out to sea, bobbing up and down like the light of a ship.

"They'll never expect us to sail along the island this way," said Halek in Nicholas's ear. "They'll be sure we would sail out to sea. If only they follow that lighted barrel, we'll get clean away."

They stood staring into the darkness, watching the light in the barrel dancing up and down.

"The wind's getting up," said Captain Harken.

At that moment, a flash of lightning zigzagged across the sky. There was a roll of thunder. Then the sky seemed to open, and the rain came down in sheets.

"They don't have storms in these islands," said Barnabas Brandy to Downalong Joe, as a great splash of water fell on Joe's head, and ran down his neck. Barnabas laughed, and Joe shook his fist at him.

"North, north-east again, Martin," cried Captain Harken. "They'll never catch us in this wind."

"North, north-east it is," cried Martin Quinn, as he swung the great wheel.

The ship swung slowly back on her course, and they ran before the storm.

They saw no more of the galleys. No galley would want to be at sea in such a wind and storm. There were white crests on the black waves, as the wind blew the water back, and the ship creaked and groaned as the sea struck her.

It was two hours before the clouds began to break, and the moon shone down again on the empty, storm-tossed sea.

Nicholas was in the bow of the ship, when Captain Harken sent for him. Nicholas made his way across the pitching deck. He was beginning to get used to the tossing ship. He found Captain Harken in the great cabin, just settling down to a meal. Barnabas Brandy was there with him, and Halek, and Martin Quinn. Tom Gold was there, too. Two men were on deck, keeping watch. The other buccaneers were below, slinging hammocks or cooking in the galley, except for Downalong Joe, who had taken Martin Quinn's place at the wheel.

"Come and join us, boy," said Captain Harken. "You must need something to eat."

Nicholas sat down at the table. He felt almost too tired to eat. It seemed very warm in the cabin, after the wind and rain on the deck. His head felt heavy. He found himself nodding, and he heard Barnabas Brandy laugh.

"Wake yourself up with some soup, boy," said Barnabas Brandy, giving him a shake. Tom set a bowl of soup in front of him, and he took a spoonful. It was very hot, and he began to feel better. He found that the others were talking about the Dragon Men.

"They'll be in all the Islands of the South by now," said Martin Quinn.

"You're right, Martin," said Tom Gold. "Do you remember what Rasha said, when he was trying to get us to join him? They've got two hundred galleys in the islands."

"I wonder where their main base is," said Captain Harken thoughtfully.

"Somewhere we can't get at them," said Barnabas Brandy. "We were lucky to get away."

Captain Harken looked across at the map on the wall of the cabin.

"We'll make for Ramir," he said. "The Dragon Men will be planning to attack our ships. We must get home and warn them."

"May they sink in the next storm!" cried Barnabas Brandy, bringing his fist down on the table.

"Well, we know what we're up against now," said Captain Harken. He looked at Nicholas. "I'm glad you're with us," he said.

"He needs to grow a bit before he'll be much use," said Barnabas Brandy.

Captain Harken shook his head. "That's where you're wrong, Barnabas," he said. "It's not <u>who</u> he is – it's <u>what</u> he is that matters. We've always been lucky, when we've had someone from The Other Side with us."

Barnabas opened his mouth in surprise. He stared at Nicholas.

"The Other Side?" asked Nicholas.

Captain Harken nodded. "That's right," he said. "You came out of that cave on the island. Quick Johnny told me. There was only one set of footprints on that beach, coming out of the cave. There were no footprints going into the cave – and no other way into it. Quick Johnny had a look. That means you came through – from somewhere else. You did, didn't you?"

"I – I think I did," said Nicholas. His eyes were closing again and he felt his head beginning to nod.

"He'll be asleep in a moment, wherever he comes from," said Barnabas Brandy. "I'll get him a donkey's breakfast, and he can bed down."

Nicholas stared at him. What did he mean by a donkey's breakfast?

"Put him in the starboard cabin," said Captain Harken.

"What?" cried Barnabas Brandy. "The cabin with the silver window? The one where Jeremy used to sleep?"

"That very one," said Captain Harken.

Barnabas Brandy rolled out of the cabin door. He was back again in a few moments with a sack full of straw.

"Here you are, boy. Here's the donkey's breakfast!" he cried cheerfully. "This way for the donkey!"

Nicholas struggled to his feet. He followed Barnabas to a door in the wall of the great cabin, on the starboard side. It opened on a little room, more like a cupboard than a cabin. There was a table in it, a chair, and a leather bucket of water, but nothing else. Barnabas dropped the sack of straw on the floor. Nicholas dropped down on it. The sack was fastened at both ends, and it made a good mattress.

Barnabas tossed a blanket over him. "See you in the morning," he said. "Or perhaps not, if you're one of Them." He shut the door.

Nicholas was too tired to think about what he meant. He lay there, staring into the darkness. There was a square window in the end of the cabin, looking out over the sea at the stern of the ship. A big ring of silver had been set in the glass. It shone strangely bright against the black of the night sky outside. Nicholas tried to remember what Barnabas had said. Something about a cabin with a silver window. That must be it. The ring was shining like silver fire. Nicholas felt that he must look at it more closely. It reminded him of something.

He stood up and took a step towards the window. The ring of silver fire grew bigger and bigger.

It seemed to be shining all around him. He felt as if he were stepping right through it.

He took another step forwards and found himself in a room, with the moonlight shining in through a window. He stood quite still, and looked around him. He was back in his own bedroom at home.

Nicholas crossed the room and climbed slowly into bed. He was still very tired. He pulled up the clothes and shut his eyes. A minute later, he was asleep.

Nicholas opened his eyes to find the sun streaming into his room. He sat up and stared around him. For a moment, he wasn't sure where he was. Then he saw his clothes lying on a chair, just as he had left them. His half-eaten apple lay on the table by his bed. It was morning, and he was in his own attic room in the house he never called 'home'.

"A dream – it must have been just a dream," he said to himself. It was just a dream. Only a dream. He felt very miserable. He looked across at the picture.

The next moment Nicholas was out of bed and across the room.

The picture had changed!

There was the silvery-white ring, just as it had been before. And there was the sea. But the ship had gone! There was no ship in the picture at all! It looked just like the sea outside the window of the cabin in *The Silver Dolphin*.

Nicholas stepped back and stared at the picture. He was sure the ship had been there, but there was no ship now.

"Nicholas! Nicholas, are you up?"

That was his mother calling from downstairs.

"Coming!" he shouted.

He pulled on his clothes slowly. He was no longer miserable. He was thinking hard. Somehow or other, he had joined that ship. And all the time he had spent on her hadn't counted at all in his life here in the town. He had been in another country. He remembered Captain Harken saying that he came from 'The Other Side'. The other side of what? Of the ring. The ring was the way through. If he had been there once, he could go again.

Nicholas suddenly felt happier than he had felt for years. He struggled into his jersey, pulled open the door of his room, and ran downstairs to breakfast, two steps at a time. He had found out the secret of the picture and the silver ring. He remembered Great-Uncle Jeremy, and laughed. He was still laughing to himself with happiness, as he opened the kitchen door, and went in to breakfast.